Library of Congress Cataloging in Publication Data

Schuller, Robert Harold.
    The greatest possibility thinker that ever lived.
    1. Jesus Christ—Person and offices. 2. Christian life—1960-. I. Title.
BT202.S375   232   73-1196
ISBN: 0-8007-0580-7

IMPOSSIBILITY THINKING

You know what that is?
It's the kind of thinking that says:
      "It's impossible!"
      "It won't work."
      "It'll never happen."
      "I haven't got what it takes."
      "Why bother to try?"
So
JESUS should have been

      the world's greatest impossibility thinker

For He had *nothing* going for Him.

JESUS was

> a member of a despised minority,
> a citizen of an occupied country,
> a nobody as far as the Romans were concerned,
> a joke to the occupying power,
> a nuisance to His fellow Jews.

There was also an inscription over him, "This is the King of the Jews" (Luke 23:38).

JESUS lived among an oppressed,
  cynical and
  embittered people!

  Taxes were oppressive.
  Freedom was unknown.
  Survival was uncertain.
  Religion was restrictive, negative, and joyless.

Yet Jesus never made an inflammatory speech,
  never organized a guerilla force, and
  never led a march on Jerusalem or Rome.

Now when he heard that John had been arrested, he withdrew into Galilee (Matthew 4:12).

JESUS inherited no illustrious name.

His father was a common laborer.
His mother was a simple, homespun type.
His uncles and aunts; who were they?
His grandparents? Nobodys!

He could never point with pride to a
prestigious address. Rather
He came from a city reputed to be culturally
deprived and morally corrupt.
"Can anything good come out of Nazareth?"
was a common expression.

*"Is not this the carpenter's son? . . . Where then did
this man get all this"* (Matthew 13:55, 56)?

JESUS was uneducated.

Whatever His schooling was, it was simple.

The only account of His writing was a note He scribbled in the sand.

He had

> No academic degrees,
>
> No certificates of special merit, award or achievement:
>
> No trophies or medals;
>
> And He never received an honorary doctorate of divinity degree!

Jesus bent down and wrote with his finger on the ground (John 8:6).

JESUS lived and died untravelled. He never visited the exciting, glamorous world outside His own country. He saw none of the sights so important to the secular world of His day. Like

> The glistening temples of Athens: with the
> Parthenon on the acropolis holding the
> golden statue of Athena; or
> Rome—with its impressive forum, colosseum,
> and theatres: or
> The marble, pillar-lined streets of Alexandria.
> Or the spectacular city of Ephesus!

All He saw was people: lonely, hurting, sick, depressed, fearful, troubled hearts!
It made Him cry!

And He went about all Galilee, teaching in their synagogues and preaching the gospel of the kingdom and healing every disease and every infirmity among the people (Matthew 4:23).

JESUS never became an intimate friend of men of power and influence.

> He had no "big connections"
> V.I.P.'s did not seek Him out.
> Had He ever been asked for letters of
> character reference—who could He list?
> No peer professors; famous authors;
> powerful politicians; ranking generals;
> or lordly churchmen.
>
> He couldn't have been a name-dropper
> if He wanted to! (Except to say—as He
> did—that He and God were very close.)

And as he was walking in the temple, the chief priests and the scribes and the elders came to him, and they said to him, "By what authority are you doing these things, or who gave you this authority to do them" (Mark 11:27)?

9

JESUS had no organization.

His followers were men with

> broken speech,
> rough hands, and
> cracked fingernails.

They were
> unpolished, uncultured, unlettered
> and ignorant failures,

In many ways, and in critical times, they
proved to be
> unstable,
> uncertain,
> undependable and
> disappointing.

And he came to the disciples and found them sleep-ing, and he said, ". . . So, could you not watch with me one hour?". . . . leaving them again, he want away and prayed the third time . . . (Matthew 26:40, 44).

Yes,
JESUS knew

> ingratitude,
> rejection,
> misunderstanding, and
> betrayal!

JESUS—by all the psychological laws of human development, should have lived and died a

> judgmental,
> frustrated,
> critical,
> angry,
> unbelieving,
> cynical,
> rebellious,
> violence-prone,
> emotionally-deprived,
> radically militant revolutionary!

Then all the disciples forsook him and fled (Matthew 26:56).
Were not ten cleansed (Luke 17:17)?
Was no one found to return and give praise to God except this foreigner (Luke 17:18)?

11

JESUS lived and died in poverty. He had:

> No home of His own,
> No insurance policy,
> No social security card,
> No retirement plan:
> He performed a miracle to raise the money to
> pay His taxes!

> His estate? He left behind only one simple
> robe, a cheap prize to entice the gambling
> soldiers at the cross.

> So He died empty-handed—except for fresh
>   wounds—
> Leaving no fortune and no heirs.

*And Jesus said to him, "Foxes have holes, and birds
of the air have nests; but the Son of man has nowhere
to lay his head"* (Matthew 8:20).

JESUS remained unmarried,
a single adult
all His life.

So He spent His years without the
encouragement
comfort or
companionship
of a wife or children.

In a society where children were a man's
greatest treasure, He died
never having fathered
a single son or daughter.

So He died.
Childless.

*But he said to them, "I have food to eat of which
you do not know"* (John 4:32).

JESUS
Think of it: At His death

>He was only thirty-three years old!
>He was so young.
>He died before His mother!
>He was not given a half-century, or
>more, to make His mark, write His
>books, build His empire, and con-
>quer the world.

This—at least and at last—should have made
Him a
cynical impossibility thinker, crying out
through tight
lips, and bitter tears:

>"It isn't fair!"
>"I'm too young to die!"
>"Others live long and longer—why
>can't I?"
>"Oh God—give me more time!"

JESUS—

> Where was His Heavenly Father
> when Jesus needed Him most?

JESUS—

> All His life He was good, kind and loving,
> and very religious.
> Every Sabbath—He was in the synagogue.
> The Holy Scriptures—how He loved to read
> them.
> Prayer? His life was a prayer for all seasons!

JESUS—

> How He loved His Heavenly Father.
> How He trusted His Heavenly Father.
> How He served His Heavenly Father.

JESUS—

> Now on His cross—when He needs His God
>   most—
> God seems to have abandoned Him.

"My God, my God, why hast thou forsaken me"
(Matthew 27:46)?

MIRACLE OF MIRACLES!

This man Jesus turned out to be

THE WORLD'S GREATEST POSSIBILITY THINKER!

No founder of any religion ever used the word *possible* more than Jesus did!

> ". . . for with God all things are possible" (Mark 10:27 KJV).

> The things which are impossible with men are possible with God (Luke 18:27 KJV).

> All things are possible to him who believes (Mark 9:23).

> Father, all things are possible . . . (Mark 14:36).

> If you have faith as a grain of mustard seed, you will say to this mountain, "Move . . ." and nothing will be impossible (Matthew 17:20).

> ". . . with God nothing shall be impossible" (Luke 1:37 KJV).

> With men it is impossible, but not with God" (Mark 10:27).

> ". . . but with God all things are possible" (Matthew 19:26).

To **JESUS**

Every problem was a possibility in disguise.

Sickness—was an opportunity for healing.
Sin—was an opportunity for forgiveness.
Sorrow—was an opportunity for compassion.

Personal abuse was an opportunity to leave a good impression and show the world how possibility thinkers react!

And he said to him, "Truly, I say to you, today you will be with me in Paradise" (Luke 23:43).

To **JESUS**

Every person was a goldmine of undiscovered
hidden possibilities!

Peter? A tough-talking fisherman:
> But—he could make a great leader
> of a great new church.

Mary Magdalene? A common prostitute:
> But—she could become a sensitive,
> sweet soul. She could one day anoint
> His body for burial.

Matthew? A vulgar materialist:
> But—he had possibilities to become
> a great writer! Even the gospel!

No wonder Jesus rushed to meet the out-cast,
riff-raff of humanity!

*And when Jesus came to the place, he looked up and
said to him, "Zacchaeus, make haste and come
down; for I must stay at your house today"* (Luke
19:5).

18

To **JESUS**

The important fact about you and me
       is not that
       WE ARE SINNERS
       But that
       WE CAN BE SAINTS.

So Jesus never called any person a sinner! He became angry only with religious people who made people feel they were miserable, guilty sinners.

Instead Jesus rushed to build—in the worst of sinners—a belief that they, too, could be saved for inspiring service!

"You are the salt of the earth . . ." (Matthew 5:13).
"You are the light of the world . . ." (v. 14).
"Follow me and I will make you fishers of men" (4:19).

19

So
JESUS proclaimed the greatest possibility:

The immeasurable

MERCY
OF
GOD

He said to them, "Those who are well have no need of a physician, but those who are sick; I came not to call the righteous, but sinners" (Mark 2:17).

To **JESUS**

the whole world was
       jammed,
       pregnant,
       loaded,
       bulging, with
              untapped,
              undiscovered,
              undetected

POSSIBILITIES!

*Then he said to his disciples, "The harvest is plenti-
ful, but the laborers are few; pray therefore the Lord
of the harvest to send out laborers into his harvest"*
(Matthew 9:37, 38).

*For God so loved the world that he gave his only Son
that whoever believes in him should . . . have eternal
life* (John 3:16).

JESUS really believed in the
supreme possibilities!

Jesus preached these grand possibilities:

> Man *can* be born again!
> Character *can* be changed!
> You *can* become a new person!
> Life *can* be beautiful!
> There *is* a solution to every problem!
> There *is* a light behind every shadow!

. . . with God all things are possible (Matthew 19:26).
. . . whoever believes in him should . . . have eternal life (John 3:16).
Jesus answered him, "Truly, truly, I say to you, unless one is born anew, he cannot see the kingdom of God (John 3:3).

Yes,
JESUS had an unshakable faith in these ultimate
possibilities:

> God exists!
> Life goes on beyond death!
> Heaven is for real!
>
> He was prepared to prove it:
> by dying—and rising again!

He saw the possibility of
> ultimate justice!
> So
> He had as much to say about hell
> as He did about heaven.

"O death where is thy victory?
O death where is thy sting?"
Thanks be to God, who gives us
the victory through our Lord Jesus Christ (I Corinthians 15:55,57).

JESUS

Saw the possibility of heaven and hell in eternity.

He also saw the possibility of a transformed world—

here on planet earth.

He was impressed by what the world could become—

never depressed by what the world was.

He truly believed in the possibility of transformed lives.

He truly believed that common people can become

uncommonly powerful.

He knew without a shadow of doubt that ordinary persons

could become extraordinary persons if they could

become possibility thinkers.

So He would give self-confidence to inferiority-complexed people.

He would make it possible for guilt-infected, failure-plagued, problem-swamped persons to start loving themselves and stop hating themselves!

"Go into all the world and preach the gospel to the whole creation" (Mark 16:15).

24

What enormous self-confidence this great Possibility Thinker had! Listen to what Christ said:

"I am the good shepherd" (John 10:11).

"I am the door; if any one enters by me, he will be saved . . ." (John 10:9).

"I am the bread of life . . ." (John 6:35).

"I am the vine, you are the branches. He who abides
in me, and I in him, he it is that bears much fruit . . ." (John 15:5).

"I am the way, and the truth, and the life; no one
comes to the Father, but by me" (John 14:6).

"I am the resurrection and the life; he who believes
in me, though he die, yet shall he live . . ." (John 11:25).

Then came the end. He was accused of stirring up the people. He was placed on trial. He was charged with blasphemy. Did He not claim to be the promised Messiah? At least, did He not allow people to get the impression that He was the Son of God? In His public trial He was challenged to deny His deity, to withdraw His blasphemous statements, and clear up the confused minds of the simple people who believed Him to be God visiting earth in human form.

But He could not tell a lie, so He remained silent. The verdict was predictable: death by crucifixion! A crowd gathered to see how a possibility thinker dies. How did He die? He died seeing and seizing the possibilities of the moment! He practiced what He had preached all His life! He turned the hell into a heaven.

For here was His chance to save the soul of a lost thief who was being crucified beside Him.

". . . today you will be with me in Paradise" (Luke 23:43).

Here was His chance to teach the world how forgiving God can be!

"Father, forgive them; for they know not what they do" (Luke 23:34).

26

This was a spectacular opportunity to dramatically teach all men of all ages to come that death can be a grand reunion with God!

So His last spoken words were loaded with great expectations. *"Father, into thy hands I commit my spirit"* (Luke 23:46)!

There was a final gasp—and He was gone. The Roman commander in charge of the execution turned away—converted on the spot, he was overheard saying, *"Certainly this man was innocent"* (Luke 23:47)!

The body was taken down and sealed in a tomb. Then it happened! Easter! He was resurrected. He came back to life again.

Why do we believe this fantastic tale? Because of the incredible change in His followers. They saw Him alive again. Where they were cowards, they became fearless proclaimers in the city streets—in daylight! Where they were impossibility thinkers—they became possibility thinkers!

THINK NOW ABOUT
YOUR PERSONAL
POSSIBILITIES

Today, twenty centuries later, Christ literally lives in millions of human beings all around the world! By His death He solved His greatest problem. What was that? He could only be in one place at a time. Now, through the power of His Holy Spirit, He is able to live in millions of lives all around this world! Think of the possibilities:

Christ can infiltrate
      any race,
      any religion,
      any community,
      any country!

THE GOOD NEWS IS—
CHRIST CAN LIVE IN—
EVEN YOU!

That is what it is all about!

BEING A CHRISTIAN
IS
offering yourself to Him

Your mind—for Christ to think through,
Your heart—for Christ to love through,
Your lips—for Christ to speak through,
Your hands—for Christ to touch through!

Just imagine what possibilities for exciting living this opens up to you!

It is no longer I who lives but Christ who lives in me (Galatians 2:20).

If Christ can live within you then it is possible for you, too,

> To—Turn your problems into opportunities!
> To—Tackle your opportunities and succeed!
> To—Dream great dreams and make them come true!
> To—Switch from jealousy and self-pity to really caring about others who are much worse off than you are.
> To—Pick up the broken hopes and start over again!
> To—See great possibilities in those unattractive people!
> To—Become a truly beautiful person—like Jesus!

I can do all things in him who strengthens me (Philippians 4:13).

YOUR PRAYER FOR A NEW AND EXCITING LIFE

Jesus Christ—I've come to see that many things are possible that I never before believed were possible.

I believe it's possible—that You were sent by God into the world to be my Saviour. I accept You now.

I believe it's possible—eternal life!

I believe it's possible—that Christ is alive this moment and trying to penetrate my life through my brain as I read these words!

I believe it's possible—for His Holy Spirit to live within me! I confess my sin. I ask Christ to save me. I invite Him to come into my life. I believe it's possible!

Amen.